discover countries

Germany

Camilla de la Bédoyère

WAYLAND

First published in 2009 by Wayland

Copyright © Wayland 2009

Wayland
Hachette Children's Books
338 Euston Road
London NW1 3BH

Wayland Australia
Level 17/207 Kent Street,
Sydney, NSW 2000

Editor: Susan Crean
Designer: Paul Manning
Consultant: Rob Bowden

Produced for Wayland by
White-Thomson Publishing Ltd

www.wtpub.co.uk
+44 (0)845 362 8240

British Library Cataloguing in Publication Data

De la Bedoyere, Camilla
Germany. - (Discover countries)
1. Germany - Geography - Juvenile literature
I. Title
914.3

ISBN-13: 9780750257985

Printed in China
Wayland is a division of Hachette Children's Books
an Hachette UK company
www.hachette.co.uk

All data in this book was researched in late 2008
and has been collected from the latest sources available at that time.

Contents

Discovering Germany

Germany is a large country at the centre of Europe. It is more than twice the size of the US state of California and has the largest population in the European Union. Germany shares borders with nine other countries. It has one of the world's strongest economies, and it is highly respected around the globe for the quality of its engineering.

A country is born

Germany was once a region of many individual cities and states that ruled themselves. Each area had its own customs, traditions and laws. In 1871 they were united as a single nation. German people call their country Deutschland.

A nation divided

Germany fought and lost in both the First World War and the Second World War. In 1949, after the Second World War, the nation was divided into East Germany and West Germany.

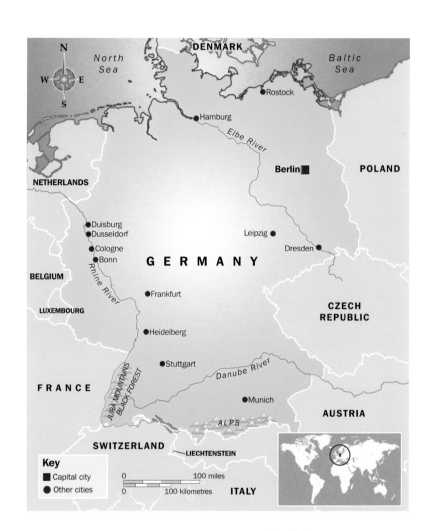

DID YOU KNOW?
In 1961 East Germany built a wall across Berlin. It stopped people moving to West Germany. The Berlin Wall was knocked down in 1989. Pieces of it are still sold as souvenirs.

East Germany was ruled as a communist state, while West Germany became a republic. The country was reunified in 1990, and became the Federal Republic of Germany.

Germany today

Germany has the world's third-largest economy, and most Germans enjoy a high standard of living. The nation is divided into sixteen states, each with its own elected government. Germany's central government is a federal republic and is led by the chancellor. The chancellor is elected every four years.

German people are known for their contributions to art, books, music, engineering and philosophy. They have experienced centuries of turmoil and war, but today live in a peaceful nation.

Germany Statistics

Area: 357,021 sq km (137,846 sq miles)

Capital city: Berlin

Government type: Federal republic

Bordering countries: Austria, Belgium, Czech Republic, Denmark, France, Luxembourg, Netherlands, Poland, Switzerland

Currency: Euro €

Language: German

▼ Neuschwanstein Castle is a royal palace in the German region of Bavaria. It was built from 1869 to 1892.

Landscape and climate

There are huge snowy peaks, vast green plains and dense forests in Germany. The landscape is also shaped by farms and towns.

Lowlands and highlands

Germany has three main regions: the plains, the uplands and the highlands.

The highlands are located in southern Germany and include part of the Alps, Europe's largest mountain range. The spectacular Black Forest covers 6,000 sq km (2,320 sq miles) in the south-west highlands. Dense woodlands cloak the mountains, creating stunning scenery and making it a popular area with tourists. The River Danube begins in the Black Forest and flows eastwards for 2,850 km (1,770 miles), reaching its mouth at the Black Sea. It is Europe's second-longest river, after the Volga.

The uplands of central Germany are high, flat-topped areas with steep sides, called plateaux. The uplands are known for their great beauty, with fast-flowing rivers, small mountains and wild woods.

The northern plains make up half of the country. This region has been eroded by glaciers and rivers over thousands of years, creating large, sweeping, flat areas.

⬤ The green countryside and forests of Bavaria are overlooked by the Alps.

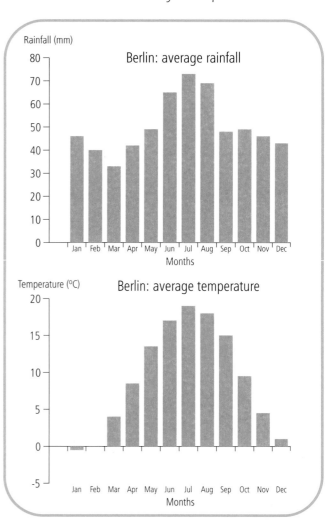

Berlin: average rainfall

Rainfall (mm)

Berlin: average temperature

Temperature (°C)

The soil is not very fertile, so much of the plains farmland is used for grazing cattle and sheep.

The Rhine

The Rhine is Germany's most important river. It flows from the Alps northwards. Industrial towns and ports were built along the Rhine, including Worms, Bonn, Cologne and Düsseldorf. For centuries people have travelled along the Rhine, trading their goods.

Seasons of sun and snow

Germany has a temperate climate. It has four seasons and snow is common in winter, especially in the mountainous highlands in the south. The plains benefit from mild winters and regular rainfall. This makes the north particularly suitable for farming.

▼ The small town of Lorch is just one of many settlements that have developed along the banks of the River Rhine.

Facts at a glance

Land area: 349,223 sq km (134,836 sq miles)

Water area: 7,798 sq km (3,011 sq miles)

Highest point: Zugspitze 2,963 m (9,721 ft)

Lowest point: Neuendorf bei Wilster -3.5 m (-11.5 ft)

Longest river: Rhine River 1,390 km (865 miles)

Coastline: 2,389 km (1,484 miles)

DID YOU KNOW?

The Black Forest is famous for its wooden cuckoo clocks, which have been made in the area since the 1740s. The world's largest cuckoo clock is in the Black Forest town of Schonach.

Population and health

Germany has a population of around 82 million. The population grew rapidly after the Second World War, but now it is falling. By 2050 Germany's population is expected to drop to 74 million.

Germans today are having fewer children than people did in the years following the Second World War. As a result, the German population is ageing, and there are more Germans older than 65 than people younger than 15.

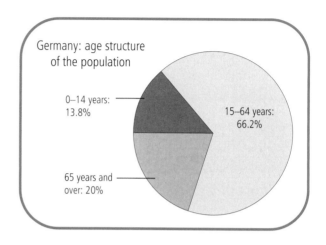

Germany: age structure of the population

0–14 years: 13.8%

15–64 years: 66.2%

65 years and over: 20%

Migration

Recently, the German government and businesses invited foreign workers to come to Germany. This is because the falling population has meant there are fewer people who can work. From 1950 to 1955, about 55,000 people migrated into Germany. From 2000 to 2005, that figure jumped to 200,000.

In the 1960s, the government invited 'guest workers' from Turkey to undertake unskilled jobs that no one else wanted. Many remained and set up their own communities. There are now around 2.5 million Turks living in Germany.

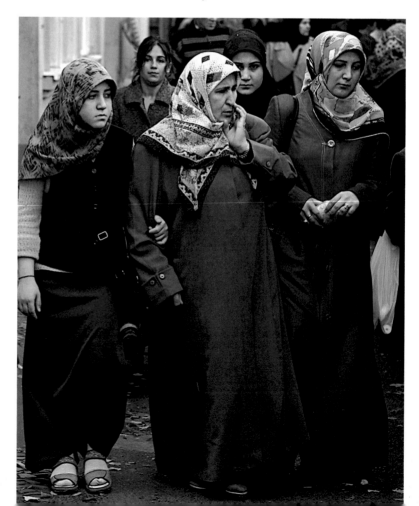

⯅ Turkish women walk in a street market in Berlin's Kreuzberg district, where many Turks live.

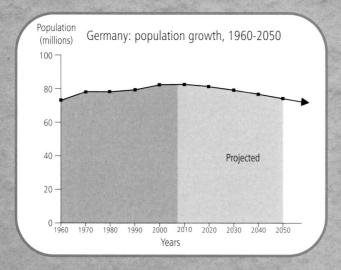

Population (millions)

Germany: population growth, 1960-2050

100

80

60

40

Projected

20

0

1960 1970 1980 1990 2000 2010 2020 2030 2040 2050

Years

Healthy lives

A German born today can expect to live to about the age of 80. The German people benefit from good living conditions and a national healthcare system.

The main causes of death in Germany are heart and circulatory diseases. The next most common cause of death is cancer.

▶ Residents of a care home for elderly people enjoy an aqua gym fitness class.

DID YOU KNOW?
In 1901, a German scientist called Wilhelm Conrad Röntgen discovered x-rays. Doctors around the world use these invisible rays of light to detect and diagnose diseases.

Facts at a glance

Total population: 82.4 million

Life expectancy at birth: 79.1 years

Children dying before the age of five: 0.4%

Ethnic composition: German 91.5%, Turkish 2.4%, other 6.1% (mostly made up of Greek, Italian, Russian, Serbo-Croatian, Polish, Spanish)

Settlements and living

Around 75 per cent of Germany's population lives in towns or cities, rather than rural areas. This is mainly due to Germany's industrial past, during which people moved from rural areas to towns and cities to find work.

Urban life

Cities provide Germans with better access to jobs, shops, schools and entertainment than rural areas. They also have better facilities such as hospitals and transport systems.

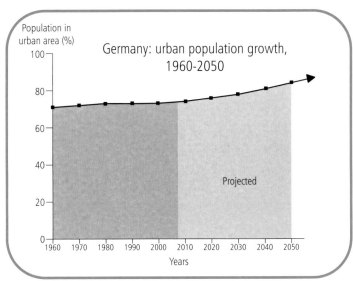

Germany: urban population growth, 1960-2050

Population in urban area (%)

Projected

Years

Cities

Germany's capital city is Berlin. Before reunification there were two capitals: Bonn in West Germany and East Berlin in East Germany. Large parts of Berlin were destroyed in the Second World War, but it has since been rebuilt. The city has a population of around 3.4 million people, and it is an important place for business and cultural activities.

🔻 Old and new buildings are found side by side in Berlin. The church on the right was damaged in World War II.

Other large cities in Germany are Hamburg, Munich, Cologne and Frankfurt. Between them they accommodate around 4.6 million people.

Where people live

Most Germans rent their homes, which may be flats or houses. Forty per cent of people own their own home. However, people in eastern Germany are more likely to live in rural areas and rent their homes than people in western Germany.

Many small towns can be found throughout Germany. They often contain old buildings built in a traditional style. Heidelberg, for example, is an historic town near the River Rhine which dates back to the 12th century. Every year it attracts around 3.5 million visitors who come to see its old buildings. These include Germany's oldest university, the University of Heidelberg, which was founded in the 14th century.

DID YOU KNOW?
German place-names give clues about an area. Towns near mountains may have 'berg' at the end of their name, e.g. Gutenberg, which means 'good mountain'. A village name often ends in 'dorf' – the word for a small settlement.

▽ Heidelberg is popular with tourists, who like to visit the Old Town district of shops, winding roads and historic houses.

Family life

In Germany, as in many other European countries, family life has changed greatly in recent years. More women work outside the home than ever before, and couples have fewer children than in the past.

Looking after family

Most German children have parents who both work outside the home. Children help out around the home and are responsible for getting themselves ready for school.

Elderly members of the family are sometimes cared for at home, although Germany has a good welfare system. It provides care for people who need it, such as the elderly and disabled.

▼ German families enjoy spending leisure time together. Here, a father and son canoe on a lake in Bavaria.

Getting married

Marriage rates have fallen in Germany and unmarried couples often live together. Around 25 per cent of all German children are born to parents who are not married. On average, people who do marry are aged between 25 and 30. As the number of marriages has gone down, the number of divorces has gone up. Many German couples decide not to have children, and when they do, they are likely to have only one or two.

Time together

The majority of German people believe that being part of a family helps them to be happy. Most young Germans say they have a good relationship with their parents and 73 per cent of all Germans aged 18 to 21 still live at home.

▼ Elderly people in Germany enjoy a high quality of life. Here, two German women sit on a bench in a meadow in Stuttgart.

Religion and beliefs

Religious beliefs are important to most Germans, and research shows that almost half of them believe in God. Most Germans describe themselves as Christians. However, the number of Muslims and Jews in Germany has increased recently due to immigration.

The Christian Church

Until about 500 years ago most Europeans were Catholic. In 1517 a German priest, Martin Luther, wanted to reform, or change, the Catholic Church. He disapproved of the way some of the priests behaved and what they preached to their congregations.

Luther's actions led to a huge change in religious practice. The period became known as the Reformation and the Protestant, or Lutheran, Church was created. Protestantism spread through Europe – and beyond. Today, most Germans describe themselves as Christians and are either Catholic or Protestant. Less than 20 per cent of them, however, go to church regularly.

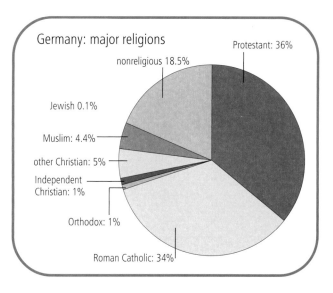

Germany: major religions

- Protestant: 36%
- nonreligious 18.5%
- Jewish 0.1%
- Muslim: 4.4%
- other Christian: 5%
- Independent Christian: 1%
- Orthodox: 1%
- Roman Catholic: 34%

Protestant Church Day was held in the German town of Hanover in 2005. Around 400,000 people attended.

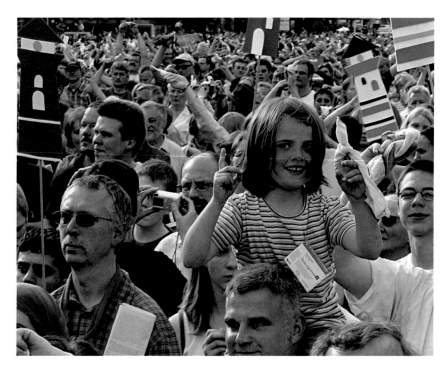

Festival time

The two most important festivals in Germany are the Christian festivals of Easter and Christmas. Celebrations also take place every year before Lent, the period that leads up to Easter, and people dress up to take part in street carnivals. These festive occasions are most common in Catholic parts of the country, especially the southern regions.

The first carnival in Cologne took place in the 14th century. Today, carnival-goers put on fancy dress costumes, paint their faces and follow decorated floats as they parade through the town. People on the floats throw lollipops and sweets into the crowd as they pass.

▼ Christmas is eagerly anticipated by German children. Shop windows are decorated to delight and entice passers-by.

DID YOU KNOW?

A number of Christmas traditions began in Germany, including Christmas trees, Advent calendars and Santa Claus.

Education and learning

German children start school when they are six, and most of them stay in education until they are 18 years old. Education and training are considered very important in Germany.

Schools

Eighty per cent of German children aged three to six go to *Kindergarten*. After *Kindergarten*, children move up to *Grundschule* – primary or first school – until they are ten. From the ages of 10 to 15, Germans are educated at a *Hauptschule* (middle school). Most schools are open from 8 am until lunchtime. Students then spend the afternoon doing homework or sports.

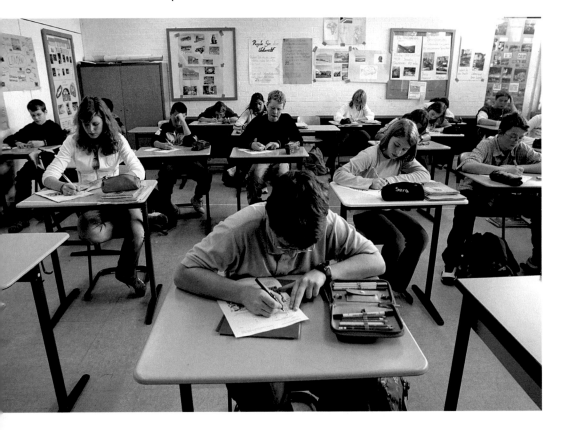

◀ Teenage students study German language in class.

Learning to work

By the age of 15 or 16, German students are expected to have decided which type of career they would like. They choose their high school according to their talents and interests.

Some students for example, might attend a *Berufsschule* (vocational school) where they take lessons and have on-the-job training for careers such as nursing, catering and plumbing. Others attend *Realschule*, where they train to work in businesses such as banks, hotels and shops. A *Gymnasium* is a school that educates students who are most likely to go to university. These students aim for careers in professions such as medicine, accountancy, law and teaching.

Lifelong learning

The German government encourages adults to return to college to learn new skills. People who cannot find jobs because they are unskilled are given vouchers. These can be exchanged for training at local colleges and universities.

Students who are learning to become bakers are shown how to make pastries and cookies.

Employment and economy

Germany has Europe's biggest economy and is one of the world's most successful trading nations. Germany is successful because it exports more than it imports. In other words, it sells more goods than it buys – and this makes wealth.

Where people work

Almost all working Germans are employed in industries and services. Industrial jobs include making goods in factories, such as cars or computers. Service jobs include working in shops, offices or in public services such as transport, health and education. Today, less than 3 per cent of all working Germans are employed in agriculture, forestry or fishing.

Germany: economic growth, 1980-2006

Economic growth (%)

Years	Economic growth (%)
1980	1.4
1985	2.3
1990	5.3
1995	1.9
2000	3.2
2005	0.9
2006	2.8

DID YOU KNOW?

Germany has one of the world's biggest economies. In 2007 the German economy earned US$6.1 million every minute. That's more than US$100,000 a second!

The city of Frankfurt is one of Europe's most important financial centres. Many banks are located here.

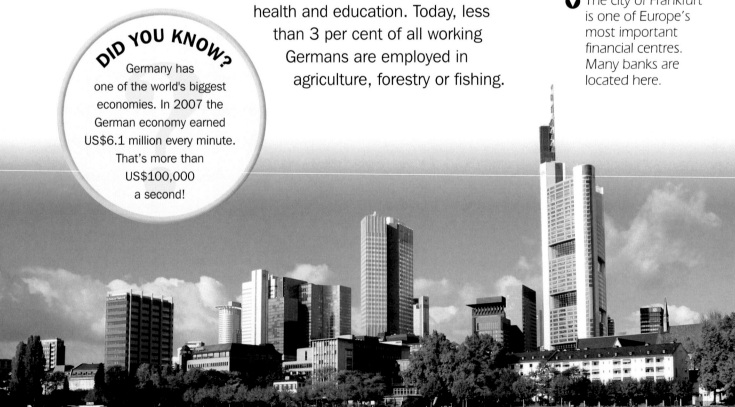

Unemployment

Germany has had a problem with unemployment since East and West Germany were reunified in 1990. Creating a new country involved joining different political and economic systems into one. Many people lost their jobs.

The German government gives unemployed people welfare benefits they can use to pay for food, housing and other essential items while they look for work.

Women at work

German unions are powerful, but they have not been able to help women to gain the same employment rights as men. On average, German women earn 22 per cent less than men who do the same job. As in many other countries, German women are also less likely to hold senior jobs.

► Car manufacturing is important in Germany. An average of 550 new cars are collected from this giant car storage centre in Wolfsburg, Germany, every day.

Facts at a glance
Contributions to GDP:
agriculture: 1%
industry: 30%
services: 69%
Labour force:
agriculture: 3%
industry: 33%
services: 64%
Female labour force:
45% of total
Unemployment rate: 9%

Industry and trade

Germany is one of the world's leading exporters because it produces high-quality goods. Around one-third of all the goods that Germany sells abroad goes to France, the US and the UK.

Secret of success

Many German factories employ experts in mechanical engineering to produce goods such as cars, ships and machinery. Electrical engineers make products such as mobile phones, televisions and computers. The success of German manufacturing is partly due to the high skill level of German workers, who excel in design and technology.

Germany's position in the centre of Europe has helped it become a successful trading nation. Germany has a good transport system and its rivers, canals, roads and railways are used to carry goods to neighbouring countries.

DID YOU KNOW? German electrical engineers wanted to improve sound quality on a telephone line. In 1987 they discovered a new way to store sound. It was the beginning of the MP3 format.

▼ Hundreds of containers are loaded onto a ship in a German port. From here they can be transported around the world.

Raw materials

Substances that are used to make other goods are called raw materials. Germany has some raw materials, such as coal, salt and potash (a fertilizer). However, it has to import most of the raw materials it needs for manufacturing. Iron is imported to make steel, while oil and gas are imported to provide energy.

Energy supplies, such as oil and gas, are expensive to import. German companies are researching better, cleaner ways to generate their own energy, such as hydroelectricity, solar power and wind power.

Coping with change

When West Germany and East Germany reunified in 1990, many businesses suffered, especially in the eastern region. Factories that made steel and textiles struggled to make money. Many of them closed down because they could not produce goods more cheaply than factories elsewhere in the world. Since then, German industries have had to concentrate on developing new products, especially computers and other electrical goods.

⬤ Steel is produced at a large industrial centre in Duisburg, on the River Rhine.

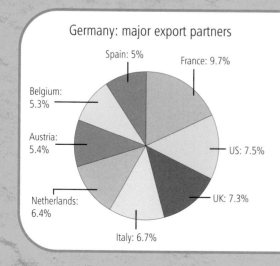

Germany: major export partners

- Spain: 5%
- France: 9.7%
- Belgium: 5.3%
- Austria: 5.4%
- Netherlands: 6.4%
- Italy: 6.7%
- UK: 7.3%
- US: 7.5%

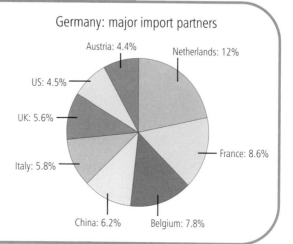

Germany: major import partners

- Austria: 4.4%
- Netherlands: 12%
- US: 4.5%
- UK: 5.6%
- Italy: 5.8%
- France: 8.6%
- China: 6.2%
- Belgium: 7.8%

Farming and food

Farming in Germany has changed since the 1980s because many small farms have been merged to make bigger ones. Large farms are more productive, which means they can grow more food and make more money.

On the farm

Most of Germany's agricultural land is used to grow cereals or as pasture for grazing animals. The most common crops are wheat, barley, corn, rye and sugar beets. In addition, hops are grown to make beer, and grapes are grown to make wine. German farmers usually grow more food than is needed by their German customers, so the extra produce is sold to other countries.

Facts at a glance

Farmland: 35% of total land area

Main agricultural exports: Cheese

Main agricultural imports: Livestock and crops, cheese, wine

Average daily calorie intake: 3,490 calories

▼ Once harvested, these grapes will be used to make German wines.

Forestry

Around one-third of Germany's land is covered with forests, and some of these are grown especially for the timber trade. Timber is wood that is used for making things, such as furniture and paper. Germany is one of Europe's largest producers – and users – of timber.

A feast of flavours

Germany is a nation of regions, and each region has its own style of cooking. Pickled fish, for example, is popular in the north, meat loaf is popular in southern areas, and doughnuts are loved by Berliners. Some international foods originally came from Germany: hamburgers are named after the German town of Hamburg, and frankfurter sausages came from Frankfurt.

German specialities include sauerkraut (pickled cabbage), pumpernickel (rye bread) and bratwurst (sausages). Another speciality is apple strudel, a pastry made with apples, cinnamon and raisins.

DID YOU KNOW?
Germany imports around 500,000 tonnes of cheese every year, but exports even more – around 700,000 tonnes. German cheese is sent to more than 60 countries worldwide.

▶ Traditional German sausages are served on a bed of sauerkraut. The German word for sausage is *wurst*.

Transport and communications

Germany has excellent transport systems, including railways, roads and shipping. People and goods are able to move easily around and through the country. Many German transport systems link up with those of neighbouring countries, and this helps to make travel through Europe faster, safer and cheaper.

Road and rail

After reunification, the railways of West Germany and East Germany had to be modernized and a single railway system, the Deutsche Bahn, was created. Around 350,000 people travel long distances by train every day, some of them on the Inter City Express trains which can travel at up to 280 kph (174 mph).

Facts at a glance

Total roads: 231,500 km (143,847 miles)

Paved roads: 231,500 km (143,847 miles)

Railways: 48,215 km (29,959 miles)

Major airports: 66

Major ports: 8

▼ Inter City Express (ICE) trains were first developed in the 1980s. ICE trains run to Paris, Brussels, Zurich and Amsterdam.

Waterways

Germany has around 7,500 km (4,600 miles) of waterways, including rivers and canals. They carry around one-quarter of all Germany's freight.

The Rhine is one of Europe's most important waterways. It has been used to transport goods for hundreds of years – even the Romans had a fleet of boats on the river. Parts of the Rhine have been straightened to make water transport easier, and canals connect the river to German towns.

Keeping in touch

Before reunification, East German telephone systems were poor, and it was not unusual for people to wait 12 years to get a phone installed. Since the 1990s, the German telephone system has been improved, to become one of the most advanced in the world.

In 2001 one-third of Germans used the Internet, but now it is available to two-thirds of the population – and that figure is growing. Mobile phones are called Handys in Germany, and seven in 10 people own one.

⬤ The city of Rostok lies where the river Warnow meets the Baltic Sea. It is an important shipyard and port.

DID YOU KNOW?
An enormous, water-filled bridge connects two German canals. The Magdeburg Water Bridge is Europe's longest water bridge, at 918 km (570 miles). It was built from 24,000 tonnes of steel.

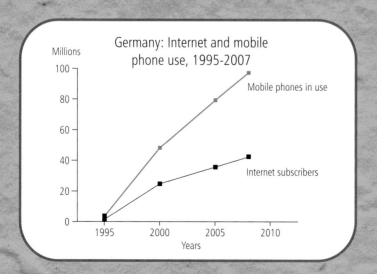

Germany: Internet and mobile phone use, 1995-2007

Millions

Mobile phones in use

Internet subscribers

Years

Leisure and tourism

During their leisure time, Germans enjoy pastimes such as sport and travelling abroad. In addition, Germans spend time relaxing by visiting art museums, listening to music and reading books.

Country of culture

Germany has a rich cultural past. Beethoven, Bach and Handel are three German-born composers whose music has been enjoyed for 300 years. Albrecht Dürer is regarded as one of Europe's greatest artists. He came from Nuremberg, and his paintings are on display in German art galleries. Karlheinz Stockhausen was born in Cologne in 1928. He became an important creator of modern classical music.

The Brothers Grimm lived in the 1800s and wrote fairy tales, such as Snow White and Rumpelstiltskin, which are still popular with many children today.

The city of Berlin hosts open-air concerts.

A sporting nation

Football is Germany's favourite sport, and people enjoy both watching it and playing it. The German football team has won the World Cup three times, and Germany hosted the World Cup in 1974 and 2006. Other popular sports include gymnastics, tennis, sailing, hiking and cycling.

Germany for tourists

Nearly 20 million people travelled to Germany for holidays in 2007. Most of those visitors came from the Netherlands, the US and the UK. Tourists come to Germany to see sights such as historical towns and to visit shops and museums. Some of the most visited destinations include Berlin, the Black Forest and the Bavarian Alps, where winter sports such as skiing and snowboarding are popular.

▼ Hiking through Germany's beautiful landscapes is a popular pastime.

DID YOU KNOW?

Nearly 80 per cent of Germans holiday abroad every year. Most Germans take at least two holidays each year, usually in Germany or within Europe.

Environment and wildlife

Germany is a developed country, and much of its natural habitat has been affected by building, farming and industry. Like many other countries, Germany is now working to reduce the effects of these activities on the environment.

Cleaning up

Rivers, land and ocean waters have been contaminated by chemicals and other polluting materials. This problem is especially severe in the former East Germany. Burning coal to generate electricity caused acid rain, and some forests have been damaged by acid rain, particularly in south-east Germany and the Black Forest.

A number of chemical factories along the Rhine have been closed because of the chemical pollutants that they were releasing into the air and water. The German government now has strict rules about pollution, chemical safety and waste disposal.

DID YOU KNOW?
Before 2002 the River Elbe was known as Europe's dirtiest river. After a long clean-up programme, the Elbe was declared clean enough for swimming – and a party was held to celebrate in July 2002.

⬤ At this glass recycling facility in Koblenz used glass is sorted, melted and processed so it can be turned into new glassware, such as bottles.

Renewable energy

Germany is committed to reducing its contribution to global warming, which is partly caused by the burning of fossil fuels such as oil and coal. The government aims to reduce the nation's carbon emissions by 40 per cent between 1990 and 2020 by using renewable energies, such as solar and wind power. Wind is Germany's most important renewable energy, and there are more wind turbines here than in any other country in the world. At the moment wind turbines supply around 5 per cent of all electricity in Germany.

National parks

Germany has many National Parks where habitats such as forests and marshlands are protected. Harz National Park is home to a number of lynx. These big cats became extinct in the Harz Mountains more than a hundred years ago, but they have recently been reintroduced to the area.

▶ About 5 per cent of Germany's energy needs are provided for by wind power.

Glossary

Catholic largest branch of the Christian community, led by the Pope

climate normal weather conditions of an area

communism economic and political system in which all people are meant to have an equal share of a nation's property and wealth

communist state form of government that operates under a system whereby all property is publicly owned

contaminated soiled, infected or made dirty

culture way of life and traditions of a particular group of people

economy way that trade and money are controlled by a country

eroded worn away by wind, water or ice

export good or service that is sold to another country

federal republic a government made up of states that are united by a central power

fertile good for growing crops, especially in large quantities

GDP total value of goods and services produced by a country

glacier large, slow-moving body of ice found on land

habitat the place, or type of place, where a plant or animal normally lives

hydroelectricity electricity that is generated using the power of falling or fast-moving water

immigration movement of people to a foreign country to live

import good or service that is bought from another country

landscapes physical features (such as mountains, rivers and deserts) of a place

manufacturing making products, usually from raw materials

migration movement of people from one place to another

philosophy study of basic ideas about knowledge, right and wrong, truth, God and the meaning of life

pollution substances that contaminate or poison, such as chemical waste

republic a system of government in which people elect officials to make decisions on their behalf

reunified brought a divided country together again

rural to do with the countryside or agriculture

temperate climate a mild climate that is neither extremely hot nor extremely cold

textiles fabric or cloth

unemployment being without paid work

unions organizations of workers who join together to protect their rights

urban to do with towns and town life

welfare system a system where the government takes responsibility for people's wellbeing, e.g. giving money to the unemployed, helping the elderly and disabled and providing healthcare.

Topic web

Use this topic web to explore German themes in different areas of your curriculum.

History
Find out what you can about communism. Which countries are no longer communist, and how many still have this political system in place?

Geography
Germany has areas of karst landscape. Find out what this means, and identify three other countries that have this feature.

Science
There are plans to reintroduce wolves to Germany. Why are some species of animal, such as lynxes and wolves, reintroduced to an area – and what problems might they cause?

Maths
The German currency is the Euro (€), which is used in many other European countries. How much is 10€ worth in your currency? Calculate the value of 5€ and 100€.

Germany

English
Write a fairy story in the style of the Brothers Grimm. Imagine your reader is a child aged six to eight years old.

Citizenship
Germans are part of the European Union. Find out when this organization began and write a list of all of its current member nations.

Design and Technology
Explore the role German inventors Karl Benz and Gottlieb Daimler played in the invention of the car, and the contributions that modern German designers have made to the car industry.

ICT
Use the Internet to find some simple German recipes. Print them out, and use them to make simple German food such as apple strudel, warm potato salad or pretzels.

Further information and index

Further reading

Germany (Country Topics), Rachel Wright and Ting Morris (Franklin Watts 2007)
Germany and the Germans (Focus on Europe), Anita Ganeri (Franklin Watts 2004)
The European Union Today, Simon Ponsford (Franklin Watts 2007)
Germany (Food and Celebrations), Sylvia Goulding (Wayland 2008)

Web

www.about-germany.org
This site contains fast facts and information on German places and culture.
http://news.bbc.co.uk/1/hi/world/europe/country_profiles/1047864.stm
This is the BBC news page for Germany with links to recent events and background information on politics.
www.germany-tourism.de
The official government information service has good information about Germany.

Index